The

Sum

of

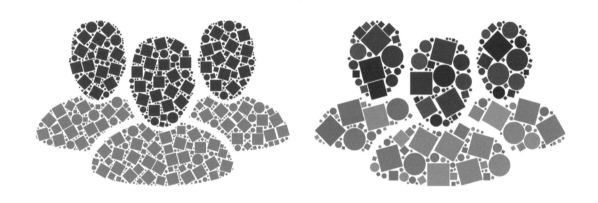

Who

You

Winifred Smith Eure

Are

To order additional copies of this book, contact:
Xlibris
844-714-8691
www.Xlibris.com
Orders@Xlibris.com

ISBN: Softcover   978-1-6641-4878-9
         EBook   978-1-6641-4877-2

Print information available on the last page

Rev. date: 12/16/2020

Dedication

I dedicate this book to the memory of my beloved three brothers: Reginald Smith Sr., Dennis Terry Smith I, and Wayne Stephen Smith. Eternal rest and peace to the three of you.

Love,Sis

Contents

Introduction

We all have our own unique view of the world around us. Equally unique is our view of ourselves within it. We act and react. We see. We hear. We use all our senses. In this book, I have tried to offer up my interpretations the best way I know how.

I am asking you to be vigilant and to read with an open mind and heart. For each of us, the sum of our experiences makes us who we are.

A Matter of Faith

COVID-19 perplexed us all.
Will it still be with us in the fall?
We ask what changes we must make—
A new normal for all our sake.
How we shop, how we work and play,
How we eat and interact from day to day.

COVID-19 known as the "beast."
Will it reappear or cease?
Scientists research a cure—
A vaccine that will work for sure.
Will the economy survive
In the wake of jobs lost and lost lives?

COVID-19 said to be like the flu—
A recurring danger to me and you?
Answers we seek will come
When the Creator's will is done.
A new day is certain to appear.
A time for absolute faith, not fear.

A time to stand together, not to weep.
A time to reflect and a time to reap.
A time to know more and a time to
achieve.
A time to build and believe
That this nation we occupy
Is like the stars in the sky.

So COVID-19 no matter how unkind,
You are most unlikely to outshine
Hopes and dreams of those home and
abroad
Who yearn to conquer you with the help
of the Lord
Whose hand is both mighty and gentle,
Defeating you while lifting hearts,
plentiful.

Why Me, Lord?

He heard a still small voice.
It seemed to whisper in his ear.
He thought it one from the past
Until it became crystal clear.

The words softly flowing
Telling him to beware.
Someone had a message
For him to hear.

Having reclined
In his favorite chair,
A friend approached
With a matter so near.

Tears filled his eyes.
His throat weakened too.
He knew then and there
His son had not pulled through.

This tragic event
That had taken a life
Pierced his soul
Like a stiletto knife.

His son—only son—
Murdered attempting flight
In a choke hold by a white officer
In the heat of the night.

A Mosaic in Motion

Young black boys
And young black girls,
I want to encourage you
While you're in this world.

There are more beautiful black faces,
More vibrant black voices
In every domain than ever before—
More meaningful choices.

The classrooms, the libraries,
The information per diem,
Family vacations,
Historical and cultural museums.

The outreach of churches
And other programs in communities
Offer much more today
In the way of amenities.

You can dream.
You can soar.
You can open
That door.

No room for fear of failure
Or low self-esteem.
No measuring yourself by standards
Of people you think supreme.

Believe you are beautiful.
Believe you have heart.
Believe you have gifts.
Believe you have a part

To play in your journey.
For every day that you're here,
You're a mosaic in motion—
A sum of everything you hold dear.

Superheroes

When your children
Read a superhero story,
They read of his superior strength
And his victories and glory.

Of his ability to perform,
His ability to save,
His popularity—
What movie audiences rave.

He's usually quite handsome
And has a love interest
A rival who wants
To put his skills to a test.

No doubt, this makes
For a fun and amazing narrative.
But if realistic,
Let's stay in perspective.

The most endearing quality
Of most these men
Is their kindness and generosity
For the people for whom they win.

The heart of a superhero
Supersedes all else.
When post conversations arise,
They should focus on that self.

Caring, helping, triumphs for those
Who need dire assistance
Are what children should take away
Without resistance.

The influence of stories
And movies of such
Should be to make better people
Of the children we love so much.

Christmas Times

Will Christmas be a time
That comes but once a year?
Or will it be a season that lives
In our hearts throughout the year?

Can we put behind us
The unforeseen sorrows
That find ways to our doorstep
And threaten our tomorrows?

Will Christmas be a time
That keeps us focused on what we can
get? Or will it be a season
When giving is a number 1 hit?

Can we triumph over the mundane
Day-to-day worry,
Share love and joy
Without hopelessness, just be merry?

Will Christmas be a time
Of just another twenty-four-hour day?
Or a happy recollection of Christ's birth
And second coming on the way?

Yes, Christmas can be times
Like these and more.
Let the blessings of the season
Resonate with us forevermore.

Merry **Christmas**

Have You Ever?

Have you ever been offended
Hurt to the core?
Have you cried yourself to sleep
And locked the door?

Have you ever been humiliated
Wrongfully shamed?
Unthoughtfully called out
Of your family birth name?

Have you ever known failure
By far missed the mark
To reach a dream
That had long been in your heart?

Have you ever been afraid
To try that one new thing
That appears so fulfilling
It could make your heart sing?

Have you ever traveled to another
Country, looked in the eyes of a stranger,
And saw there a glimpse
Of some familiar anger?

If you can lay claim
To any of these,
It's because you are human
And need God's peace.

When the Heavenly Father made you,
He knew your life's course.
He wanted you to grow
And find joy in the Lord.

Joy that abides and doesn't die—
Eternal love deeper than seen by the eye.
It pervades your living not with perfection
But with faith, grace, and daily reflection.

Can-Do Power

Can you sing a solo
Recite a scripture
That's not too hard to learn?

Can you say a prayer
Get out the house and get some air
That is God-inspired?

Can you prepare a balanced meal
Dare walk on a shoe without high heels
That brings you comfort and joy?

Can you lend a helping hand
Sit down and create a plan
For someone else in need?

Can you manage a smile
Utter friendly words a while
That will lift and encourage another?

Can you make a phone call
Throw a bowling ball
Do something to make yourself feel better?

Can you water some flowers
Calm a crying infant
Be a nurturer when needed?

Can you read a novel
Drive a car
Do something that might take you far?

Can you paint a picture
Write a poem
Be creative when not on the go?

Can you iron a shirt
Sew the hem of a skirt
With a touch of domestic simplicity?

Can you fix a broken toy
Babysit a girl or boy
Repair and give care all in one?

Are these some
Or all things you can do?
May you always remember to be glad you
are you.

Songbird

Songbird
Beautiful songbird
Singing his praises

Whether a joyous gospel
Or baptismal hymn,
Songbird sing his praises again and again.

Light up the room. Permeate this space.
Let your voice resound
In this sacred place.

Songbird
Echoes of the past
And present connecting at last

Beautiful songbird
In your colorful choir robe
Songbird, young and old

Your notes, your pitch,
And your lyrics too
You have touched many hearts that were
sad and blue.

Songbird, yes, give the glory to God
In your sight and sound.
Songbird, sing softly, sing loud.

Lest We Forget Our Maker

The too sugary and extra salty foods
The inevitable drama of the daily news
The novels and music that call some back
to best forgotten yesterdays.

The sum of all these ways
We treat body, mind, and soul
And yet complain if we don't feel whole.

Best careful of what and how much we
take in
For many of us
Are well past 3×10.

Guilt, anxiety,
And doubt
Weariness all about?

Why feed on these?
Rather get on your knees
Ask God to make a brand-new you.

Peace of mind, self-control
Faith-filled
And never too old to learn.

Young at heart,
Not falling apart
At the seams.

A wiser, more certain, yet humble walk
Is what I aspire to, not just bold talk.
If I can please the Alpha and Omega,
Let me be always ready to meet my Maker.

My Brothers' Children

My brothers—
They made
Such beautiful children!

Their hearts
Warm and
Filled with love.

They give and share
With open hands,
Wear smiles with a light from above.

They talk
And teach.
They plant and reap.

They've birthed
Girl and boy,
Experienced sorrow and joy,

Known victory
And defeat.

What I like most
About them all—
They've remained innately sweet.

Printed in the United States
By Bookmasters